LIAM BLAKE

SHRINES

LIAM BLAKE

SHRINES

INTRODUCTION
FINTAN O'TOOLE

First published in 2001 by Real Ireland Design Limited ©.
27 Beechwood Close, Boghall Road, Bray, Co. Wicklow, Ireland.
Telephone: +353 1 2860799. Fax: +353 1 2829962.
web: www.realireland.ie   e-mail info@realireland

Photography Liam Blake ©.

Text Fintan O'Toole ©.

Book & jacket design Brian Murphy.

Extract from the poem 'The statue of the Virgin at Granard speaks' from 'The man who was marked by winter' (1991) by Paula Meehan, by kind permission of the author and The Gallery Press, Loughcrew, Oldcastle, County Meath, Ireland.

ISBN 0-946887-13-6

British Library Cataloguing Publication Data.
A catalogue record for this book is available from the British Library.

The great traditional singer and song collector Frank Harte, sings a ballad called The Finding of Moses, believed to have been written by the 19th century street singer Michael Moran, otherwise known as Zozimus. The song begins with a conventional if demotic account of the Biblical episode it narrates:

On Egypt's banks contagious to the Nile
The oul' Pharaoh's she went to swim in style.

The sense of time and place are clearly established, Egypt, the Nile, the Pharaoh. It is, as you might expect with a Biblical story, a long time ago and far away. As the song progresses, however, its co-ordinates subtly shift. The story is still Biblical, still happening on the banks of the Nile many centuries before Christ. But it is also unfolding here and now, in the Dublin inhabited by the passing people whose farthings and ha'pennies the composer was trying to seduce from their pockets. When the mysterious baby is presented to the Pharaoh, he explodes in outrage at the apparent abandonment:

Bedad, says the Pharaoh, I'll search every nook
From the Phoenix Park down to Donnybrook
And when I catch hold of the bastard's father
I will kick him from the Nile down to the Dodder.

The frame of mind in which the Dodder is within kicking distance of the Nile and the Pharaoh is a Dublin hard chaw is what characterises folk religion. Especially among the poor and the unhappy, the desire to transform the plain familiarity of the local world into the sacred realm of a holy land has always been strong. When the founder of modern Irish trade unionism, James Larkin railed at the employers with the warning "You'll crucify Christ in this town no longer", he was tapping into that desire. When enslaved blacks in the southern United States transformed the Mississippi into the Jordan, when William Blake sang of building Jerusalem in England's green and pleasant land, when Rastafarians in Jamaica imagine themselves as the Jews in captivity in Babylon, they are expressing it in their own terms.

In Ireland, from the beginning of Christianity in the fifth century AD, this folk religion has always been there, sometimes supporting the official church, sometimes in competition with it. Part of the reason for the relatively easy triumph of Christianity on the island was that it generally sought to assimilate rather than to uproot the complex nature of the religion that the first missionaries found there. The church, fitted itself snugly into an existing social structure that was highly localised and tried to appear familiar rather than strange. Saint Patrick's legendary use of the shamrock to explain the concept of the Holy Trinity is itself an image of how what was already there was simply given a new gloss. Sacred mountains like Croagh Patrick in County Mayo became places of pilgrimage that persist to this day. Sacred springs at which the water spirits were honoured became, with the addition of a crucifix or the image of a saint, holy wells. The ancient spirits accepted their fate with remarkable serenity. The old magic (the cure of blindness or warts or infertility) stayed in place, happily interwoven with Christian devotion. The priests, being local men, had no great desire to interfere with immemorial traditions.

Their own faith, besides, leaned towards pantheism. Until relatively recently, the Irish church was inclined to see the evidence of God in his creation: the trees, the hills, the sky, the mountains. With that closeness to nature came a deep sense of locality. However far they wandered, Irish monks tended to retain that sense of the local. Marginal comments on German monastic manuscripts complain that when they were drunk the Irish monks started to insist that Jesus was really Saint Patrick and Mary really Saint Brigid.

Thus, the notion that holy places might be fields and woods as well as churches and cathedrals had a particular appeal. And that appeal was almost certainly deepened by the long period of oppression in the 17th and 18th centuries when the Catholicism to which the majority of the Irish clung was penalised. Unable to build churches or, at times, to hear Mass in view of the authorities, worshippers moved outdoors.

Some of the wayside shrines and grottoes in Liam Blake's wonderfully evocative pictures probably recall half-forgotten memories of times when these places had to become holy ground. More generally, the habit of mind which sees nothing disrespectful in having the stations of the cross in a wood or a shrine in a block of flats probably results from this period in which the great outdoors was the only church.

It was not accidental, however, that the creation of a tightly disciplined Irish Catholic church after the traumatic famine of the 1840s was marked by an explosion of church building. Institutions like to have people where they can see them. The folk religious practice that allowed the church to survive persecution was also worryingly independent of clergy, bishops and doctrinal control. As the church struggled to create a respectable modernity for its flock, it also became rather uneasy about the shrines and holy wells. With their vestiges of paganism and their touch of wildness (pilgrimages to holy wells often took on a dangerous air of sociability) these places were slightly beyond the bounds. Yet, the habit of assimilation was so strong that few priests or bishops actively tried to eradicate them. An attitude of wariness became the norm: watch what was happening, and, if showed signs of lapsing too obviously into superstition, take control.

This ambivalence was deepest in the mid-1980s, when statutes of the Virgin Mary at shrines all over the country began to come to life and move. The epidemic of miracles brought huge crowds to places like Ballinspittle, County Cork and Asdee, County Kerry. Unsure whether they ought to welcome the phenomenon as evidence of renewed devotion at a time when the church's political authority was beginning to loosen, or to condemn it as an embarrassing lapse into superstition, the authorities lapsed for the most part into an anxious silence.

Meanwhile, troubled people sometimes found more comfort in the lifeless statues of the grottoes and shrines than in the human face of church and State. Paula Meehan's poem 'The Statue of the Virgin at Granard Speaks' recalls the death of fifteen year-old Anne Lovett who died giving birth at the foot of the statue:

On a night like this I remember the child
who came with fifteen summers to her name,
and she lay down alone at my feet
without midwife or doctor or friend to hold her hand
and she pushed her secret out into the night,
far from the town tucked up in little scandals.....

Even as the institutional church loses its poise, the wayside images that make every small place into Jerusalem or Calvary, retain their imperturbable power to attract the yearning of troubled people. So long as the towns are tucked up in scandals, they will endure.

Fintan O'Toole

Roadside shrine near Ardara, Co. Donegal.

Saint Brigid's Well, Liscannor, Co. Clare.

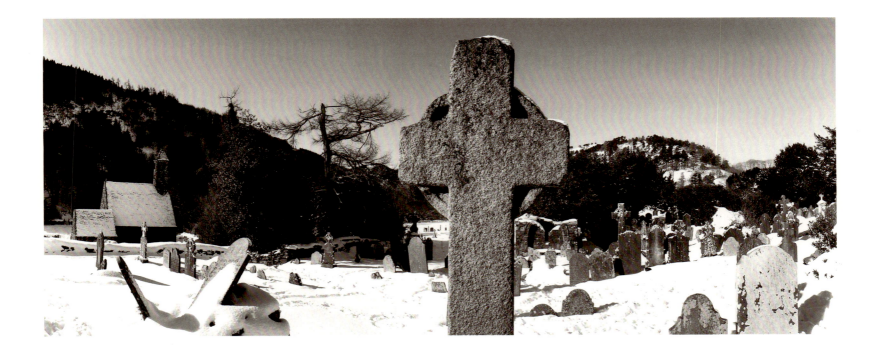

Wishing Cross, Glendalough, Co. Wicklow.

Saint Brigid's Shrine, Faughart, Co. Louth

Saint Kieran's Well, near Killybegs, Co. Donegal.

The Cranavane Holy Well, Kildavin, Co. Carlow.

Roadside shrine near Castletownbere, Co. Cork.

Urban shrine, Ringsend, Dublin City.

Shrine, O'Connell St. Dublin City.

Shrine souvenirs, Knock, Co. Mayo.

Shrine souvenirs, Knock, Co. Mayo.

Saint Joseph's Shrine, Rosbeg, Co. Donegal.

Fishermans shrine, Meenaclady Pier, Co. Donegal.

Lady of the Little Way House, Grangecon, Co. Wicklow.

Crossroads shrine, Millstreet, Co. Cork.

Saint Machain's Well, near Kilmuckridge, Co. Wexford.

Virgin Mary statue at dusk, near Westport, Co. Mayo.

Roadside shrine, Greenane, Co. Wicklow.

Crucifixion shrine, Slea Head, Co. Kerry.

The Grotto, Ballinspittle, Co. Cork.

Saint Mary's Well, Killargue, Co. Leitrim.

Saint Dahillan's Well (detail), Co. Kerry.

Crucifixion shrine, Sheeps Head Peninsula, Co. Cork.

Shrine detail, Manmore Gap, Co. Donegal.

Shrine, Manmore Gap, Co. Donegal.

Saint Patrick shrine, Tulsk, Co. Roscommon.

Stations of the Cross. Tulsk, Co. Roscommon.

Roadside shrine, Letterfrack, Co. Galway.

Mobile shrine, Lough Gill, Co. Sligo.

Winking Jesus, shop window, Clifden, Co. Galway.

Shrine, Lady's Island, Co. Wexford.

Shrine in winter, Glencree, Co. Wicklow.

Saint Chaorie's Shrine, Kilkee, Co. Clare.

Saint Brigid's Well (detail), Liscannor, Co. Clare.

The Grotto, Bray, Co. Wicklow.

Village shrine, Athleague, Co. Roscommon.

Crucifixion mural, North inner city, Dublin

Acknowledgments

This collection of photographs is a small visual record representative of the many thousands of Shrines and Holy Wells that are to be found throughout Ireland.

It was the artist Tim Goulding and his then partner Helen Strong, who about fifteen years ago suggested to me that the shrines of Ireland would make an interesting photographic project. Although I have included the occasional shrine picture in different publications over the years, it was not until more recent times that I began to bring this series of photographs together as a theme in itself.

I would like to thank Brian Murphy for his design of this book in the busy week before his marriage to Catherine Curran.

Liam Blake - 2001

Printed in Ireland by Brookfield Print.

Origination and plates: Lithographic Plate Plan.

Additional plates and notes

Frontspiece: Saint Brigid's Well, Liscannor, Co. Clare.

Photographs on pages 38 and 42 were first published in 'Shoreline' 1991

Liam Blake
Liam Blake is widely known for his colour postcards and calendars of Ireland and is the author of several photographic books.

Fintan O'Toole
Fintan O'Toole is a regular columnist with the Irish Times newspaper and is the author of several books including the 'Irish Times Book Of The Century'.